b small publishing

GROW ORGANIC EAT ORGANIC

A practical activity book for beginners

Lone Morton

Illustrations by Martin Ursell

*Thanks to Rosalie and Mark at Wave Hill Farm for all their inspiration
and commitment to organic growing*

Published by b small publishing
Pinewood, 3a Coombe Ridings, Kingston upon Thames, Surrey KT2 7JT
© b small publishing, 2001
2 3 4 5
All rights reserved.
Design: Lone Morton   *Editorial*: Catherine Bruzzone and Susan Martineau   *Production*: Olivia Norton and Grahame Griffiths

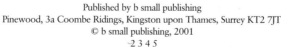

British Library Cat   ble from the British Library.

D0522907

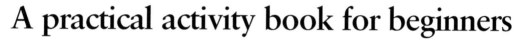

What does organic mean?

Since the 1940s more and more chemicals have been used in gardening and farming:
- chemical fertilizers to grow crops
- pesticides to kill pests
- herbicides to kill weeds

FACT: Did you know that a lettuce may have been sprayed with up to 11 pesticides by the time you eat it?

Many small farms have been replaced by enormous farms which grow just one crop on a huge area of land. This encourages pests and diseases while the chemicals can damage our land, water, wildlife and health.

Organic farmers and gardeners do not use these chemicals. They work with nature to produce their crops.

FACT: A farmer must not use chemicals on his land for four years before his produce can be labelled as organic.

Organic farmers vary the crops they grow on the same land. This helps to control the pests and diseases which attack that crop. Each crop also takes different nutrients or goodness from the soil. Changing the crops each year (crop rotation) keeps a balance of nutrients in the soil.

Organic growers make sure they feed the soil with organic compost (see page 8). They also grow 'green manures'. These are crops, like alfalfa or clover, which are grown specially to be dug back into the soil as compost. Then there is no need for chemical fertilizers.

A well-balanced organic environment encourages nature's own pest controllers too, like ladybirds which eat aphids (insect pests). There is no need for chemical pesticides.

Many people are now choosing to eat organic food and so many more farmers are changing over to organic ways of growing their crops. You can use organic methods in your gardening too. The organic way is not complicated or difficult. It is the most natural and straightforward way of raising plants.

So organic growing means:
- a variety of crops on one piece of land
- rotating the crops year by year
- feeding the soil with compost
- not using chemical fertilizers, pesticides or herbicides.

Go organic?

There is more and more organic produce available in the shops these days. The more people buy it, the more our farmers will produce it. But you can have a go at growing your own organic harvest too!

In the UK look out for these logos on packaging. They are only awarded to organic growers and producers.

Growing things is a real thrill. It's even more exciting when you can eat what you have grown. Just imagine munching into a delicious tomato and cress sandwich and drinking a yummy strawberry milkshake knowing that you have grown the tomatoes, cress and strawberries yourself. And, most important of all, you've grown them organically.

FACT: You cannot wash off all the chemicals used in conventional farming. They often become part of the cell structure of the fruit or vegetable.

Getting started

This book will introduce you to growing organically and give you some great ideas for recipes too. Sometimes you will need a bit of help from a grown-up.

Have fun experimenting and try growing a variety of things. Some will amaze you and others may fail. It's a good idea to keep a notebook so that you can record your results to help with future experiments.

Even if you don't have a garden you could use a balcony, sunny window-sills or hanging baskets to start growing your own organic food. Have a go!

Before you begin

You will need a few tools to get going. See if you can borrow them as you need them. Wear suitable outdoor clothing and footwear. It is also a good idea to wear gardening gloves to protect your hands.

Seed trays or containers
A seed tray is for sowing seeds but you can use all sorts of alternatives. See page 7.

Secateurs
Secateurs are for cutting and pruning stems and branches.

Spray bottle
A very fine spray is needed for watering your seeds and young seedlings.

Watering-can
A watering-can with a sprinkler on the spout is very important. Your plants cannot survive without water.

Trowel and fork
A hand trowel and a hand fork are probably the most useful tools in your garden, whatever its size.

Rake
A rake smooths out and levels the soil.

Hoe
A hoe is used for weeding.

Fork
A fork is used for spreading compost and for loosening up the soil. There are different sizes of fork. Use a small, light one.

Spade
A spade is used for digging – sometimes for digging holes but also for digging over the soil.

Canes and garden twine
Bamboo canes are really useful as stakes to support your growing plants. The twine is for tying plant stems to the cane.

How plants grow

Nature's cycle of life includes animals, insects, plants, soil and, of course, the sun and rain. They all play a major part in keeping the essential balance of nature. All living things depend in one way or another on the soil. The top soil, which is the first layer on the outside of the Earth, is bursting with life.

Natural life cycle

(1) Plants need light, water and warmth to grow big and healthy.

(2) In turn animals and insects feed on those plants.

(3) The animals then manure the soil.

(4) Worms and insects take the manure and other decaying matter into the soil.

(5) The worms and bacteria in the soil break down the manure into humus. This enriches the soil.

(6) The soil feeds the plants through their roots.

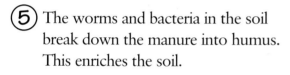

Germination is when the planted seed first starts to grow.

The roots grow down into the soil to get water and minerals to help the shoots to grow.

The shoots grow and become plants.

FACT: In 1 teaspoon of soil there are millions of bacteria.

FACT: Did you know that it takes nature 500 years to produce 25 mm of top soil?

Making your garden

You can grow vegetables and plants in pots, tubs, and even old tyres, if you are not lucky enough to have a patch of soil. The most important thing is that whatever or wherever you choose it must be in a sunny position.

Do not be tempted to plant too large a garden. The ideal plot size to begin with is 1 metre by 1 metre. If possible, ask an adult to help you erect a 1½-metre trellis at the end of your plot that faces the sun. This can be used for climbing plants such as cherry tomatoes, cucumbers and beans.

CHECKLIST
Your plot or pots need:
- lots of sunshine
- no large overhanging trees
- A tap close by
- Good soil, which you can improve with compost.

1 The first thing you will need to do is clear your garden area of weeds. You can do this either by hand or use a hoe. Try to get all of the root up, otherwise the weed will grow again.

2 When the weeds have all been removed you will then need to fork over the whole area, turning the soil to a depth of 20 cm. A good time to ask for some help!

3 Then add organic compost (see page 8) to feed the soil. Use your spade to spread about 5 cm of compost over the area. Mix it in with the fork.

4 Now pull a rake slowly back and forth to level the surface of your plot. Your garden is now ready for planting.

WEEDY TIP
Weed your garden often, as young weeds are much easier to pull out!

Planting pots, containers and window-boxes

Terracotta flowerpots look very nice but the soil in plastic pots dries out more slowly. All kinds of containers can be used to grow plants. Just remember to drill holes in the bottom for drainage. As plants in pots are growing in a more restricted place it is a good idea to use plenty of peat-free organic potting compost mixed with some good soil.

What you will need:

- containers (with drainage holes)
- broken bits of clay pots or stones
- organic potting compost and soil
- trowel

Rolled-up newspaper tied with string makes a good growing container.

Containers need stones or broken bits of clay pots in the bottom to stop the drainage holes getting blocked up with soil.

FACT: Did you know that peat bogs are places where rare and wonderful plants grow? The bogs are disappearing as peat is dug out to sell to gardeners – use peat-free composts to save the bogs.

You can use old margarine pots or cut-down milk cartons as seed trays, too. Just remember to put drainage holes in the bottom.

Even cardboard toilet roll tubes work well, if supported in another container.

Allow a 6 cm gap between the soil surface and the container rim.

When you grow tomatoes in a container it is best to grow a bush variety. One plant in a 25 cm wide pot.

During dry weather don't forget to water every day. Plants in containers dry out very quickly.

A window-box is ideal for a colourful display of flowers and herbs. Put it on the kitchen window-sill so you can reach it easily when you are cooking.

7

Soil needs compost

An organic gardener feeds the soil rather than the plants. If you produce a healthy, rich soil the plants will be able to take what they need when they need it and will not require artificial fertilizers. Buy some peat-free organic compost to start off your garden, as your compost bin will take a while to get established.

What is compost?

Composting is a way of returning dead plants and vegetable matter to the soil by letting it rot in a container. A compost bin is used to collect garden rubbish and kitchen vegetable waste. Old leaves can also be collected in a separate area (see below) to make valuable leaf mould. All these things are full of the nutrients that plants need, but you can only dig them into the soil when they are well rotted, which takes at least six months.

Leaf mould

Make a wire cage by stretching wire mesh around 4 posts pushed well into the ground. Alternatively collect the leaves in plastic bin liners and hide them away in a corner of the garden for one or two years.

Liquid feeds

You can make your own liquid feed for plants. Soak lots of comfrey or nettle leaves in a bucket of water for 3-4 weeks. Strain before using to water your plants. They love it despite the smell!

Make a compost bin

This can either be made from an old dustbin with the bottom removed (keep the lid on to keep out flies) or you can buy one from a garden centre. (Some have winter jackets to keep the up temperature.)

Keep a plastic bucket or similar-sized container in the kitchen to collect kitchen waste. Empty it into your outdoor compost bin each day.

Making compost requires moisture, warmth, air and a good balance of ingredients. Layers of kitchen waste, including crushed egg shells, vegetable peelings and tea-bags, torn or shredded newspapers (no coloured ink as it is poisonous), grass cuttings, animal manure (not cat and dog), old flowers, garden clippings, straw, and sawdust from untreated timber are all ideal. This mixture can take six months or more to become a crumbly brown compost. It will be ready at the bottom first.

You could make a wormery as well or, if you are short of space, instead of a compost bin. See page 9.

Manure

If you want to use cow, horse, chicken or rabbit manure, preferably with straw mixed with it, you must compost it in your compost bin first. It is not safe to put straight on the soil.

Make a wormery

You can recycle your kitchen waste and turn it into compost using a wormery. You will need composting worms such as brandling worms. They are also known as red or tiger worms (available from worm farms or by mail order, see page 24). They are different to the worms you have in your garden. Brandling worms love rich, organic matter and can be found in leaf mould and established compost heaps. You can buy wormeries (see page 24) but why not make your own and just buy the worms?

What you will need:

- small plastic dustbin with lid
- drill to drill holes in the dustbin
- 2-3 bricks
- gravel
- thick cardboard and scissors
- bedding: coir or shredded newsprint, or mixture of both, soaked in water
- 250-500 brandling worms
- shallow container to collect liquid

FACT: Worms breathe through their damp skin. If they dry, they die!

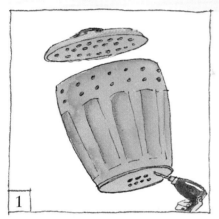

1

Ask an adult to drill a few small holes in the bottom of the bin for the liquid to drain out. Also drill 2 rows of small ventilation holes around the top edge and in the lid.

2

Place your bin outside, protected from sunlight and frost. Stand it on 2–3 bricks and place a container underneath to collect the liquid for plant food.

3

Put in a layer of gravel. Cut a circle from the cardboard to cover the gravel. Add a 10 cm layer of bedding (see 'What you will need' above).

4

Add the worms and let them settle in for 3-4 days. Cut another circle of cardboard to cover the bedding and worms. This keeps them in the dark, which they like.

Avoid meat products, onion and citrus peel.

5

Once the worms are established, lift the card cover and put in 1 or 2 handfuls of raw vegetable waste every day. It can take up to 6 months to fill a bin with compost.

Plant feed:
Use the liquid you collect to feed your plants. Dilute 1 cup of liquid with 10 cups of water.

When the bin is full of compost, scoop off the top layer, which contains most of the worms, to start again. Then use the remaining compost on your garden.

You could send off for more information and facts on wormeries (see page 24).

Sowing seeds indoors

Growing from seed is very exciting and satisfying, particularly when you see the little shoots emerging from the soil and, with your care and attention, developing into healthy seedlings. If possible buy organic or untreated seeds.

Depending on the weather and where you live, you may need to start off your seedlings indoors to avoid the danger of frost.

Use any kind of container from flowerpots and special trays from a garden centre, to old plastic yogurt or margarine pots (see page 7).

What you will need:
- containers with drainage holes
- potting or seed compost
- sieve
- selection of seeds
- shallow tray

1

Use a sieve to make a fine layer of compost over the soil.

2

Once seeds have sprouted move to a sunny position.

3

Fill a container with the compost. Use another smaller container to press the surface down gently to make it flat.

Sow the seeds about 1 cm apart. Sprinkle more compost over them until they are covered with just a very thin layer.

Stand the container in a shallow tray of water for about 10 minutes. Spray the seeds regularly, keep moist not wet.

Make a mini-greenhouse by putting your planted container in a clear plastic bag, blow in air and close with a twist tie.

Moving seedlings

Instead of thinning crowded seedlings you can move them to new containers. Use a small stick to make rows of holes about 5 cm apart. Holding on to the seed leaf (the first two round leaves to grow) put the roots and lower stem into the hole. Cover with soil and press down gently. Water and put in a light place.

Planting outdoors

When the risk of frost has passed you can move your seedlings outside to get used to the different conditions. When they are big enough they can be planted out into your garden area. Some seeds can be sown immediately in the ground outside, especially in the spring. Check the instructions on the seed packets.

Planting seedlings outside

To plant seedlings outside, dig small holes in rows in the prepared soil between 1 and 30 cm apart, depending on the plant. Tip the container to release the seedlings and soil. Lower the roots and stem into the hole. Cover with soil up to the bottom leaves.

Spread your fingers around the plant when turning the pot upside down.

1

2

3

Prepare your soil (see page 6). Use your rake to make it level. Then gently pat it flat.

Use the stick to make parallel grooves in the soil about 35 cm apart and 2 cm deep. Sow the seeds about 1 cm apart. Cover with soil.

You must water the planted area regularly, but don't drown it. As the seedlings grow they may need thinning out. Pull out the weaker ones.

basil

Label your rows of planted seeds or seedlings carefully. It is very easy to forget what you have planted! Lolly sticks are perfect.

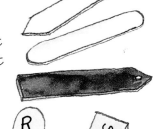

CHIVES

ROCKET

sunflower

Sow a sunflower seed

In the spring, plant a sunflower seed in a small container of potting compost. When it is approximately 25 cm high plant it outside in a sunny position. Water it every day and watch out for snails and slugs (see page 18). You will need to stake your sunflower. Tie the stem to the stake in several places to stop it falling over.

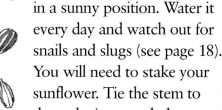

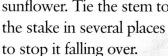

Grow food to eat

Freshly picked, organic, home-grown vegetables and fruits are delicious.
Here are a few examples of fruits and vegetables that are easy and fun to grow.

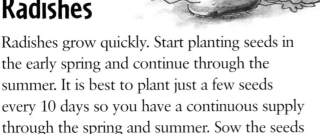

Radishes

Radishes grow quickly. Start planting seeds in the early spring and continue through the summer. It is best to plant just a few seeds every 10 days so you have a continuous supply through the spring and summer. Sow the seeds 1-2 cm deep and 10 cm apart.

> FACT: Planting the herb chervil near your radishes will make them taste less hot and deter the flea beetle.

Lettuce

To have a continuous supply of salad through the summer, sow just a few seeds and then sow again when those have germinated. Sow from early spring in trays (see page 10) and when the seedlings have 4-5 leaves plant them out in your garden. Check seed packets for spacing as different varieties vary.

Tomatoes

In the early spring buy small plants, preferably from an organic supplier (see page 24). If you are planting in pots put one plant (preferably a bush variety) in a pot at least 25 cm wide.

Fill the container with a mixture of peat-free potting compost and good soil. Push a bamboo cane in firmly and then plant the tomato plant next to it.

- Tomato plants need regular watering and a liquid seaweed or comfrey feed (see page 8) each week.
- Put a straw or newspaper covering around the plant to keep the tomatoes off the soil.
- Pick when they are bright red. See pages 20-21 for good tomato recipes.

As the tomato plant grows you will need to tie it loosely to the bamboo cane with garden twine.

Pinch out side shoots growing between the leaf and main stem.

French beans

French beans grow well in containers or out in the garden. If you are going to plant them out in the garden it is better to start them off in pots and then transplant them when they are 15 cms high. This gives them a better chance to survive the slugs who love them.

Plant beans 20 cm apart and provide bamboo canes, at least 150 cm long, to support them.
• Water regularly.
• The beans will be ready 10-12 weeks after sowing.

Cucumbers

Cucumbers grow well in containers or in the garden. Buy outdoor cucumber plants in the early spring. They will need stakes to grow up and plenty of watering.

Potatoes

Sprout a potato by putting it in a warm, light place like a window-sill. When the sprouts are about 2-3 cm long they are ready to put in the compost. Only keep two sprouts on each potato; rub off the others. The potatoes should be ready to eat in about 10-12 weeks.

The bamboo canes can be made into a wigwam shape and tied at the top with garden twine.

IMPORTANT TIP
Remember that green potatoes are poisonous so you shouldn't eat them.

What you will need:
• large pot or container
• good, rich organic compost
• 2 potatoes that have sprouted
• watering can

Shoots should face up.

1

In the spring fill the large pot one third full of compost from your bin. Put in the 2 sprouted potatoes, cover with more compost.

2

Water regularly. As they grow add more and more compost. When the pot is full leave the potatoes to flower.

3

When the flowers die stop watering. When the leaves die your potatoes are ready. Tip the pot out and see how many!

Strawberries

Freshly picked strawberries are the best!
It is really worth growing your own.

Strawberries grow well in pots or in the garden.
Buy organic strawberry plants if possible (see
page 24 for suppliers). Strawberries need well-
composted soil, careful weeding and regular
watering during dry weather, particularly if
they are in pots.

Plant 30 cm apart in spring. As the fruit ripens
put either straw or 'mats' (available from
garden centres) around each plant to keep the
strawberries clean.

After the fruit has finished, remove the old
leaves and leave the new shoots in the centre
for next year's growth. Plants will produce fruit
for 3 to 4 years but then will need replacing.

Mature plants grow
long stems, called
runners, which produce
baby plants along them.
You can either cut these
off, or pot some of them
as shown below.

Turn to page 23 and make a delicious strawberry milkshake.

Potting runners

1 nip off the rest of the runner

2

3

Fill a small pot with good garden
soil. Select a healthy looking baby
plant on a strawberry runner.

Push the base of the baby plant
into the soil.

After a few weeks, the baby plant
will have grown its own roots.
You can then cut the runner,
move the pot and plant it out.

Grow a pumpkin for Hallowe'en

As pumpkins take a few months to grow you will need to plant seeds in the spring to make sure they will be ready in time for Hallowe'en or other autumn celebrations. There is a delicious pumpkin recipe on page 22.

FACT: Did you know there are over 100 varieties of pumpkin?

What you will need:

- pumpkin seeds
- good, rich organic compost
- 9 cm wide pot or container
- trowel
- watering-can
- liquid feed (see page 8)

1. In late spring, sow 2 seeds in the pot. Keep inside in a warm spot. The plants will grow quickly.

2. Plant outside when there are no longer frosts at night. Water regularly and use a liquid feed once a week at night.

3. Only allow 2 or 3 flowers per plant to grow. As the pumpkins develop place a tile or board underneath each one to keep it clean. After you have cut a pumpkin, leave it to dry in a sunny place to harden the skin.

Mustard and cress

Planting cress is fun and it is good to eat in organic bread sandwiches. Lay a few layers of paper towel in a baking tray (or similar container), dampen with water and sprinkle with mustard and cress seeds. Place in a sunny, light position and make sure the paper always remains damp. When fully grown, cut with scissors and eat immediately.

MUSTARD AND CRESS

15

Home-grown herbs

Herbs have leaves which are heavily scented and are used to flavour food. Many herbs are also used for teas, some of which have medicinal qualities.

Some herbs can be grown from seed in the spring, and others are best bought as small plants from an organic nursery (see page 24). The herbs you grow can be used fresh to flavour many dishes or you can dry them and use them for cooking during the winter months.

Herbs can be grown very successfully in pots or you can have a herb area in your garden.

Dry herbs by hanging bunches upside down in an airy, warm place.

Make fresh mint tea
Put a handful of fresh mint sprigs in a teapot and pour on boiling water. Leave to infuse for 5 minutes and then serve. Do not add milk to herbal teas but you can sweeten them with sugar or honey if you like.

Bouquet garni
A bouquet garni is a bunch of mixed herbs used in cooking to add flavour. Make a bouquet garni by mixing together fresh thyme, marjoram, parsley and bay in small bunches and tie them together with string.

Alternatively, when they are dry put small amounts of chopped, mixed herbs in squares of muslin and tie them up with string.

Mint
It is best to plant mint on its own in a pot, or sink a pot in the ground, as it spreads rapidly.

Bay

Thyme

Tarragon

Marjoram

Sage

Rosemary

Chervil

Bouquet garni

MINT

Chives

Parsley

Grow flowers

If you grow a mix of flowers and vegetables it encourages a more natural environment for the wildlife in your garden. Certain flowers are useful as they attract insects away from vegetables, and you can eat some flowers with your salad!

What are hardy annuals?

Hardy annuals are flowers that grow, flower and die in one year. Their seeds, however, can survive through the winter and then grow into new flowers the following spring. The following are good annuals to plant in your garden:

- **Cosmos** - lovely for cut flowers.
- **French marigold** - plant these amongst your vegetables as they will keep some pests off your plants.
- **Sunflower**
- **Pansy**
- **Hemerocallis** (Day Lily)
- **Nasturtium** - both the leaves and flowers are edible, perfect for salads.

What are perennials?

Perennials die away each winter but grow again in the spring. They live for more than three years but need regular feeding with compost. The following are good perennials to plant in your garden:

- **Michaelmas daisy**
- **Hollyhock**
- **Poppy**
- **Viola**
- **Mallow**

Plant some bulbs

Autumn is the main time to plant bulbs for springtime flowering. You can either plant in pots or directly outside in the garden. Bulbs in pots make ideal Christmas gifts. Painting or stencilling terracotta pots and containers makes them look even more colourful and fun. Ceramic paint is best for clay pots.

Plant the pointed end facing up, as this is where the shoot grows.

Fill pots with potting compost. Plant bulb in a hole 3 times its own height.

Cover pots with newspaper to keep them in the dark. Put in a cool place for 8-10 weeks. This allows the roots to grow.

When shoots have grown at least 5 cm high, put the pots in a light position, like a window-sill, indoors.

Garden pests

Slugs are pests! They really are the organic gardener's worst enemy – but do not use slug pellets. These are dangerous to other wildlife, such as birds, if they eat them. Never use poisons in your garden because they will kill garden friends as well. There are other things you can do that help get rid of slugs and pests.

FACT: At night you can find up to 200 slugs in 1 square metre of garden!

PESTS
Slugs
Snails
Caterpillars
Aphids

Slugs munch everything from new seedlings to fully mature leaves. Slugs are happiest in damp, dark, well-composted conditions. They are highly active in the spring. If you go out in the evening with a torch you will be amazed at how many slugs there are out there. This is the time to collect them and dispose of them.

FACT: One slug could have 27 million great grandchildren, if they survived. **Help!**

Slug stoppers

- Try and clear your garden of slugs a week or so before planting. Make a slug trap by covering a pile of old lettuce or comfrey leaves with a tile. Every evening collect up the slug and leaf pile and add it to your compost bin. You can also take the slugs to a park to feed the ducks, or squash them.
- Use upside down empty grapefruit skins – slugs will collect underneath. Check often, particularly in the dark with a torch.
- Use yogurt pots, one third full of beer or milk, set in the ground with only the rim 1 cm above the soil. Slugs will drown. Protect from rain and change regularly.
- Broken eggshells, grit, bran, ashes are all useful for keeping slugs away from young seedlings. Sprinkle generously around each plant and replenish often.
- Alternatively, you can buy slug traps (see page 24).

Garden friends

Many useful creatures live in gardens and it really is worth being kind to them and encouraging them to take up residence. The larger the variety of plants you grow the more garden friends you will have.

Bees and butterflies

Bees and butterflies are very important as they pollinate the flowers in our gardens. Bees pick up the pollen on their hairy bodies and sticky feet and move it from flower to flower. This is called pollination. A fruit then develops around the pollinated flower seed.

FACT: Did you know that some butterflies only live for 1 week?

Honey bees

Honey bees collect the pollen and nectar from flowers and then take it back to their hives. Here the nectar is made into honey.

FRIENDS
Bees
Worms
Ladybirds
Birds
Dragonflies
Frogs and toads
Butterflies

Make a pond for frogs

Frogs and toads eat slugs so they are really good garden friends, but they do need water. Make a small pond by burying a plastic washing-up bowl in the ground. Put in some large stones, fill with water and add some pond weed, which you can buy at garden centres.

FACT: Many species of insect have become extinct because of pesticide spraying.

Feed the birds

Encourage birds into your garden with a bird table or a nesting box. Robins, for example, are very fond of fatty foods like cheese but they also like eating insects, which is good for the garden. Birds also eat slugs. Be careful to make sure that cats can't get on to the bird table!

If you are really interested in birds you could join the Wildlife Explorers. See page 24.

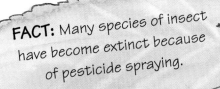

Eat the food you've grown

So you have grown some of your own vegetables and fruit.
Now it is time to make delicious meals or snacks with them.
When cooking always try to use organic ingredients if you can.

Warning!
Ask a grown-up to help with the chopping and cooking.

Wash your hands and put on an apron before preparing food.

The recipe below is a good one for using up any over-ripe tomatoes.

Tomato sauce for pasta

What you will need for 3 servings:

★ 2 tablespoons olive oil
★ 1 medium onion, finely chopped
★ 2 cloves of garlic
★ 400 g ripe tomatoes, chopped
★ 3 heaped teaspoons tomato purée
★ small bunch of basil, chopped
★ pepper and salt

- saucepan
- chopping board
- sharp knife (be careful!)
- garlic press
- wooden spoon

1

Heat the oil in the saucepan and add the onion. Using the garlic press, crush the garlic and add to the onion.

2

Cook gently for 5 minutes and then add the tomatoes, tomato purée and the basil.

If necessary add a little water.

3

Let the sauce simmer for 25 minutes, stirring occasionally. Add salt and pepper.

Garden salads

Salads can be either a main meal or a side dish. With your own home-grown lettuces, radishes, tomatoes, cucumbers and herbs, and perhaps a few extra organic ingredients, you can create some delicious and wholesome meals.

Other ingredients you can use for salads are cucumbers, olives, onions, avocado, spring onions, red and yellow peppers, even slices of orange. Be creative – it will taste delicious!

Mixed green salad leaves – mix as many different varieties of salad leaves as you have in your garden.

Add nasturtium leaves and flowers to your salad too.

Tomato, cucumber, bean and basil salad

What you will need for 4 servings:

★ 200 g green beans, topped and tailed
★ 3 medium tomatoes
★ ½ cucumber
★ small bunch of basil
★ 4 tablespoons olive oil
★ 2 tablespoons balsamic or wine vinegar
★ 1 teaspoon honey
★ salt and pepper

• small saucepan
• chopping board
• sharp knife (be careful!)
• salad bowl and servers

Add slices of mozzarella cheese or cold, cooked organic chicken to make this salad into a main meal.

1. Put the beans into a pan of boiling water and cook for 5 minutes. Drain and cool.

2. Halve and slice the tomatoes. Slice the cucumber and cut into quarters. Roughly chop the basil.

3. Put the remaining ingredients in the salad bowl and mix well to make the salad dressing. Add the chopped vegetables and toss.

21

Baked potatoes with herb filling

What you will need for 3 people:

★ 3 large potatoes
★ 250 g cottage cheese
★ 2 tablespoons natural yogurt
★ 2 tablespoons chopped fresh parsley, chives and mint
★ 1 clove of garlic, crushed
★ salt and pepper

• chopping board
• sharp knife (be careful!)
• garlic press
• baking sheet
• bowl and tablespoon

The herb filling is also very good in sandwiches.

Pre-heat the oven to 200°C/400°F/Gas Mark 6. Wash the potatoes and dry them. Prick the potatoes and ask an adult to put them in the oven on a baking sheet. They can take up to 1½ hours to cook. Mix all the other ingredients together in a bowl. When the potatoes are ready, cut open and fill with the herb filling. Serve immediately with a salad (see page 21).

Pumpkin soup

What you will need for 4 servings:

★ 1 medium onion, chopped
★ 2 tablespoons olive oil
★ 1 kg pumpkin flesh, cut into 2.5 cm cubes
★ 500 ml stock (chicken or vegetable)
★ 2 sprigs of fresh mint, chopped
★ 2 sprigs of fresh oregano, chopped
★ salt and pepper

• sharp knife (be careful!)
• chopping board
• big saucepan
• food processor

Heat the oil and cook the onions for 5 minutes, stirring continuously. Add the pumpkin and cook for 5 minutes over a low heat, continuing to stir occasionally. Add the stock and simmer for 45 minutes until the pumpkin is tender. Add herbs and salt and pepper. Use the food processor to purée the soup. Serve hot with organic bread.

WARNING
Ask an adult to remove the pumpkin skin.

Strawberries and mint

What you will need for 4 people:

- ★ 500 g strawberries, washed
- ★ 50 g soft brown sugar
- ★ grated zest of 1 lemon
- ★ juice of 1 orange
- ★ 1 tablespoon finely, chopped fresh mint
- ★ Vanilla ice-cream or natural yogurt, to serve

- · chopping board
- · sharp knife (be careful!)
- · grater or zester
- · bowl
- · spoon

Cut the strawberries into quarters and put into the bowl with all the other ingredients. Stir carefully to avoid bruising the strawberries. Cover and put in the refrigerator for 2 hours to absorb the flavours. Serve with vanilla ice-cream or natural yogurt.

Strawberry milkshake

What you will need for 1 milkshake:

- ★ 150 ml milk
- ★ 4 tablespoons vanilla ice-cream
- ★ 85 g yogurt
- ★ 100 g strawberries

- · blender
- · large, tall glass and straw

1 Put all the ingredients in the blender and turn on for a minute or two.

2 Pour into a tall glass and serve with a straw.

Useful contacts

Blooming Things
Tel: 01654 781256
Mail order company selling a wide range of organically grown vegetable and herb plants. Phone for catalogue.

The Centre for Alternative Technology
Machynlleth, Powys SY20 9AZ
Tel: 01654 702400
www.cat.org.uk
A wonderful family day out in Wales to inspire, inform and entertain all ages. Phone for leaflet and information about the centre.

Chase Organics
Tel: 01932 253666
Phone for *The Organic Gardening Catalogue* which contains everything you need for your organic garden from seeds to slug traps. Also ask for their *Ecobulbs* catalogue, full of wonderful, organically grown bulbs.

Friends of the Earth
26-28 Underwood Street, London N1 7JQ
Tel: 020 7490 1555
email: info@foe.co.uk
www.foe.co.uk
Largest environmental network in the world with over 200,000 supporters working together to help protect the environment. Young persons membership available. Quarterly magazine with a children's pull-out section called *Kids Matters,* free to members. Information booklets and resource packs on food and a wide range of environmental issues also available.

HDRA the organic organisation
Ryton Organic Gardens, Coventry CV8 3LG
Tel: 02476 303517
www.hdra.org.uk
HDRA's main aim is to promote environmentally sound, organic growing techniques worldwide. They have a wonderful selection of fact sheets on organic growing plus activity sheets for children. These are free to members.

The Recycle Works
Tel: 01200 440600
www.recycleworks.co.uk
Mail order company selling wormeries and worms plus useful books on the subject.

The Soil Association
Bristol House, 40-56 Victoria Street,
Bristol BS1 6BY
Tel: 0117 9290661
email: info@soilassociation.org
www.soilassociation.org
An organisation that campaigns for organic food and farming, and sustainable forestry.

Wiggly Wigglers
Tel: 0800 216990
email: wiggly@wigglywigglers.co.uk
www.wigglywigglers.co.uk
Suppliers of *Can-o-Worms* – a home worm composting kit. You can also buy worms and accessories for your home-made wormery. Phone for catalogue and prices.

The Wildlife Explorers
The Lodge, Sandy, Bedfordshire SG19 2DL
Tel: 01767 680 551
email: bird@rspb.demon.co.uk
www.rspb.org.uk
The Wildlife Explorers is the junior membership of the **RSPB** (Royal Society for the Protection of Birds). Members (ages 8-13) receive a bi-monthly magazine, *Birdlife*, which is full of information, activities and projects.

Young People's Trust for the Environment and Nature Conservation
8 Leapale Road, Guildford, Surrey GU1 4JX
Tel: 01483 539600
Young people's non-profit making organisation that campaigns on conservation issues. Phone for free fact sheets.